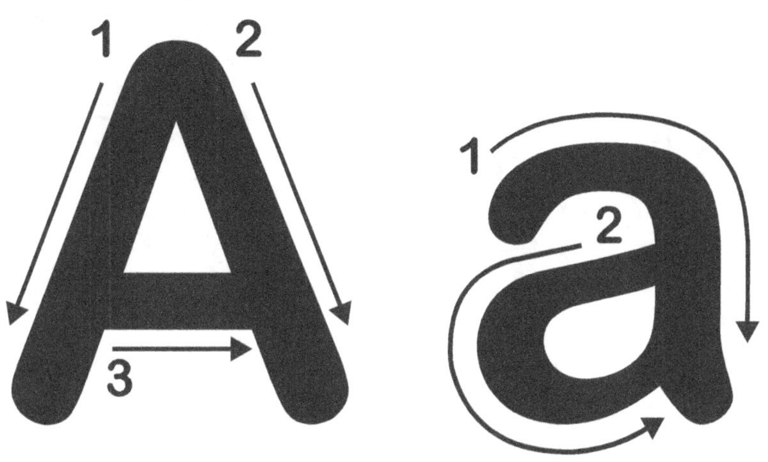

A a is for Apple

Write Alphabet

Aa   Aa   Aa   Aa

Aa   Aa   Aa   Aa

Aa   Aa   Aa   Aa

Aa   Aa   Aa   Aa

Apple   Apple   Apple

Apple   Apple   Apple

Apple   Apple   Apple

Apple   Apple   Apple

B b is for Bacon

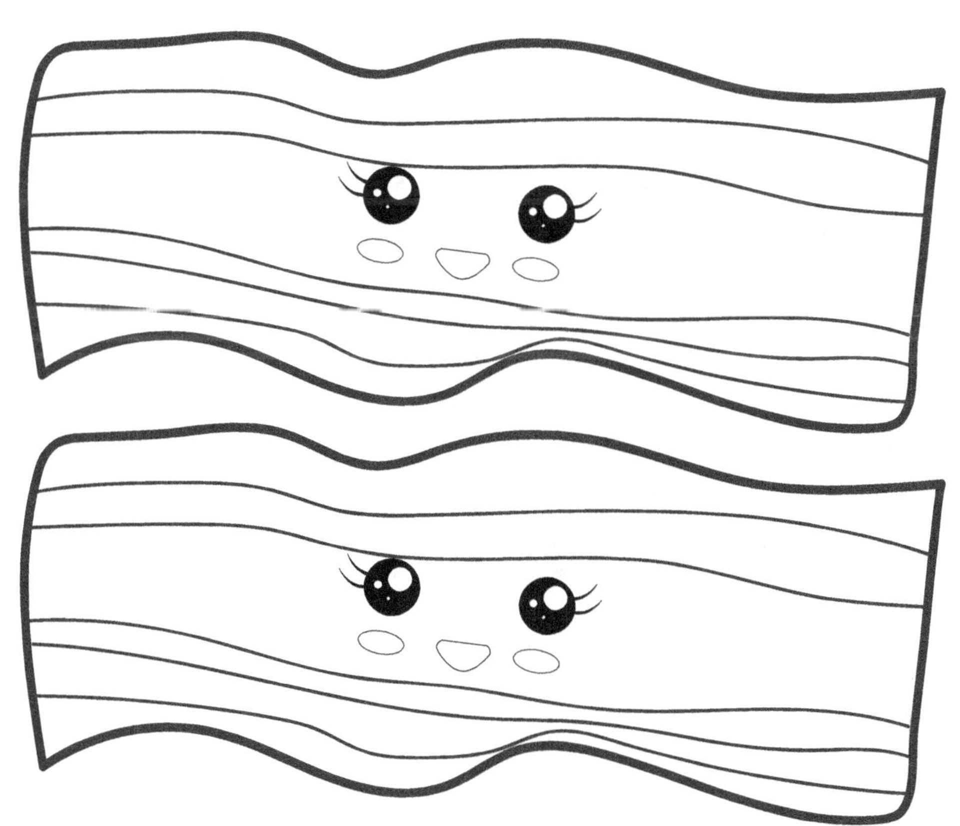

Write Alphabet

Bb   Bb   Bb   Bb

Bb   Bb   Bb   Bb

Bb   Bb   Bb   Bb

Bb   Bb   Bb   Bb

Bacon   Bacon   Bacon

Bacon   Bacon   Bacon

Bacon   Bacon   Bacon

Bacon   Bacon   Bacon

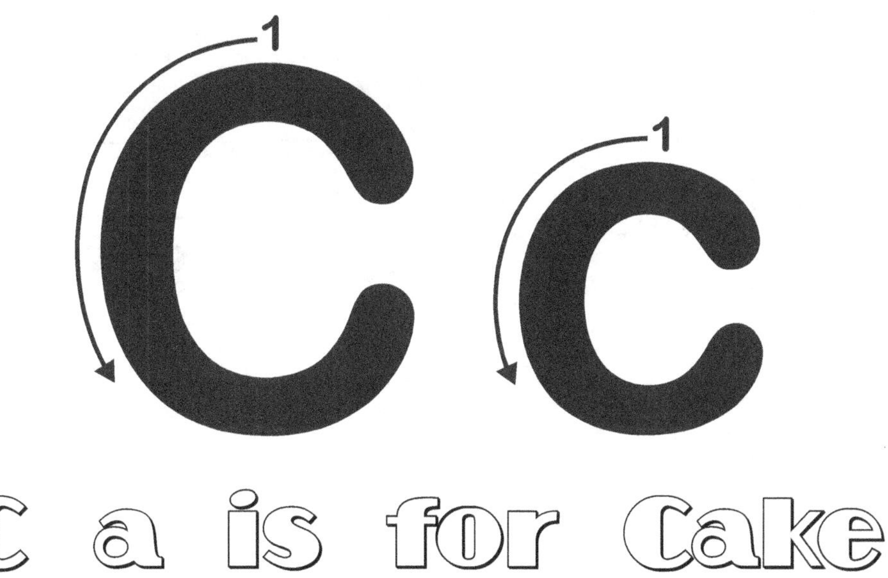

C a is for Cake

Write Alphabet

Cc   Cc   Cc   Cc

Cc   Cc   Cc   Cc

Cc   Cc   Cc   Cc

Cc   Cc   Cc   Cc

Cake   Cake   Cake

Cake   Cake   Cake

Cake   Cake   Cake

Cake   Cake   Cake

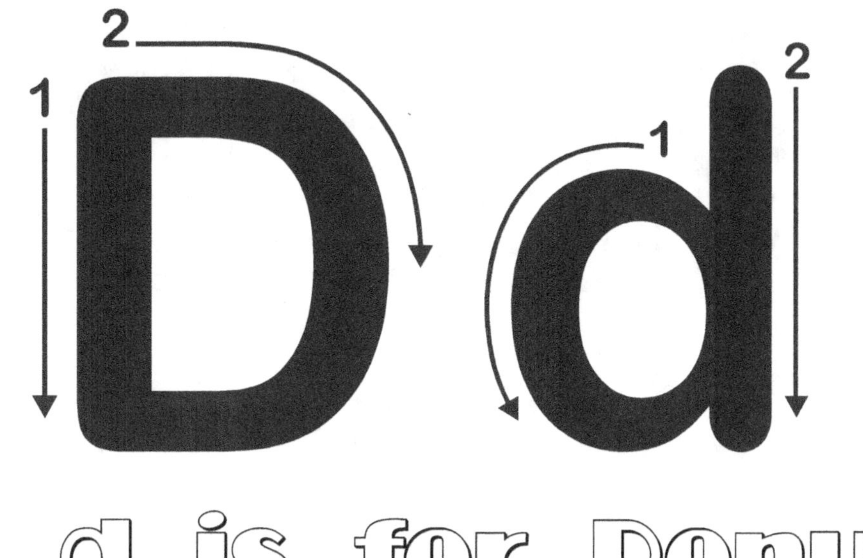

D d is for Donut

Write Alphabet

Dd   Dd   Dd   Dd

Dd   Dd   Dd   Dd

Dd   Dd   Dd   Dd

Dd   Dd   Dd   Dd

Donut   Donut   Donut

Donut   Donut   Donut

Donut   Donut   Donut

Donut   Donut   Donut

E e is for Egg

Write Alphabet

Ee Ee Ee Ee

Ee Ee Ee Ee

Ee Ee Ee Ee

Ee Ee Ee Ee

Egg Egg Egg

Egg Egg Egg

Egg Egg Egg

Egg Egg Egg

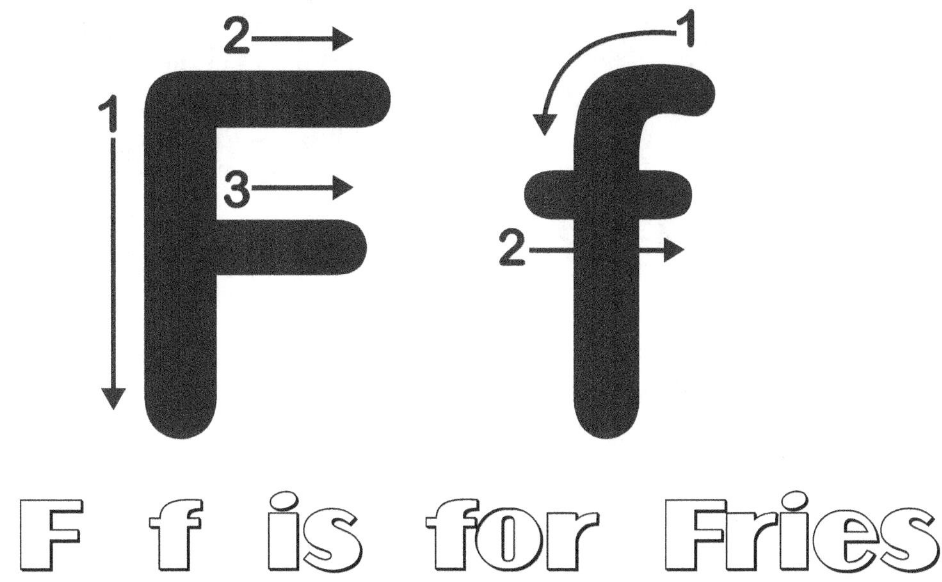

F f is for Fries

Write Alphabet

Ff Ff Ff Ff

Ff Ff Ff Ff

Ff Ff Ff Ff

Ff Ff Ff Ff

Fries Fries Fries

Fries Fries Fries

Fries Fries Fries

Fries Fries Fries

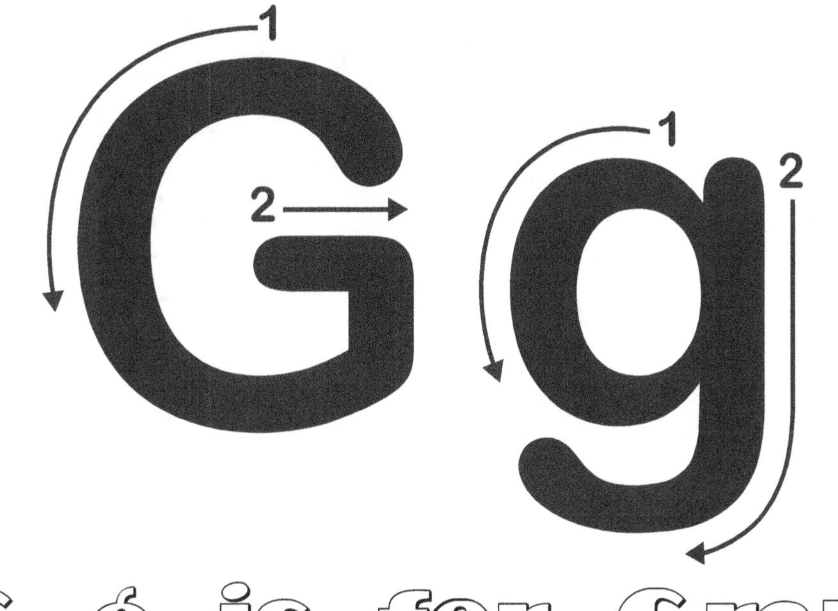

G g is for Grape

Write Alphabet

Gg Gg Gg Gg

Gg Gg Gg Gg

Gg Gg Gg Gg

Gg Gg Gg Gg

Grape Grape Grape

Grape Grape Grape

Grape Grape Grape

Grape Grape Grape

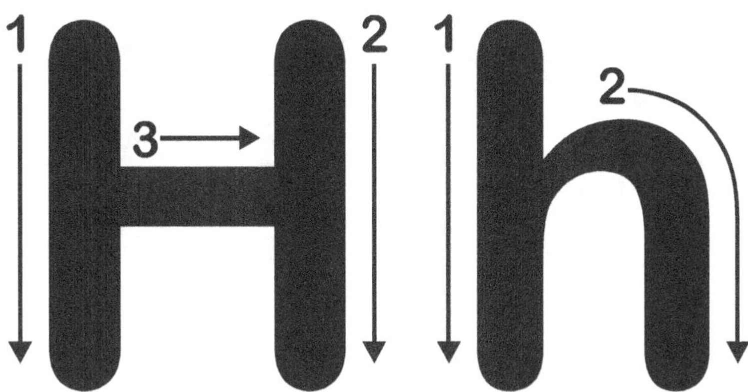

H h is for Hot Dog

Write Alphabet

Hh   Hh   Hh   Hh

Hh   Hh   Hh   Hh

Hh   Hh   Hh   Hh

Hh   Hh   Hh   Hh

Hot Dog Hot Dog Hot Dog

Hot Dog Hot Dog Hot Dog

Hot Dog Hot Dog Hot Dog

Hot Dog Hot Dog Hot Dog

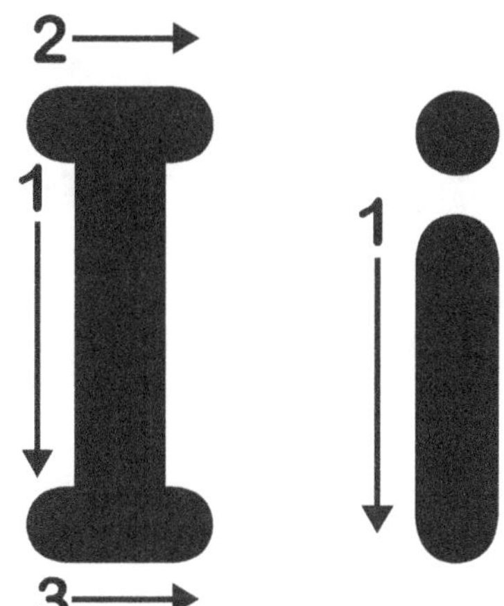

I i is for Ice Cream

Write Alphabet

I I   I I   I I   I I

I I   I I   I I   I I

I I   I I   I I   I I

I I   I I   I I   I I

Ice Cream   Ice Cream

Ice Cream   Ice Cream

Ice Cream   Ice Cream

Ice Cream   Ice Cream

J j

J j is for Jam

Write Alphabet

Jj   Jj   Jj   Jj

Jj   Jj   Jj   Jj

Jj   Jj   Jj   Jj

Jj   Jj   Jj   Jj

Jam   Jam   Jam

Jam   Jam   Jam

Jam   Jam   Jam

Jam   Jam   Jam

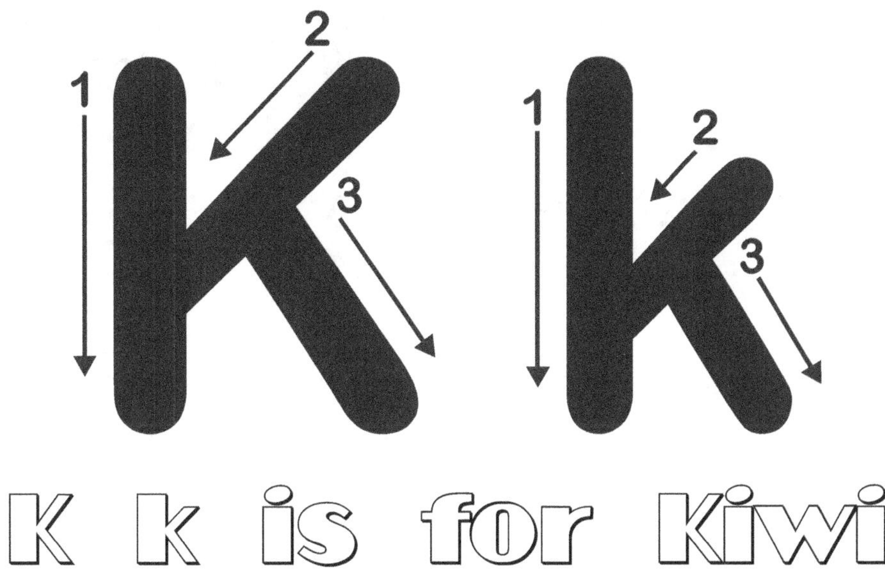
K k is for Kiwi

Write Alphabet

Kk   Kk   Kk   Kk

Kk   Kk   Kk   Kk

Kk   Kk   Kk   Kk

Kk   Kk   Kk   Kk

Kiwi   Kiwi   Kiwi

Kiwi   Kiwi   Kiwi

Kiwi   Kiwi   Kiwi

Kiwi   Kiwi   Kiwi

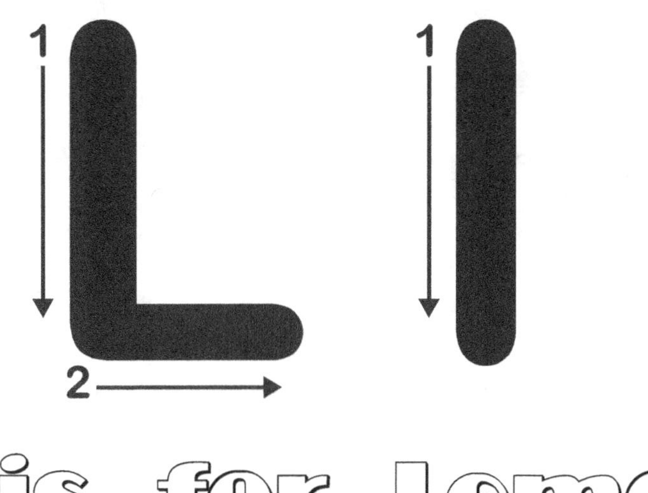

L l is for Lemon

Write Alphabet

Ll Ll Ll Ll

Ll Ll Ll Ll

Ll Ll Ll Ll

Ll Ll Ll Ll

Lemon Lemon Lemon

Lemon Lemon Lemon

Lemon Lemon Lemon

Lemon Lemon Lemon

M m is for Milk

Write Alphabet

Mm   Mm   Mm   Mm

Mm   Mm   Mm   Mm

Mm   Mm   Mm   Mm

Mm   Mm   Mm   Mm

Milk   Milk   Milk

Milk   Milk   Milk

Milk   Milk   Milk

Milk   Milk   Milk

N n is for Nut

Write Alphabet

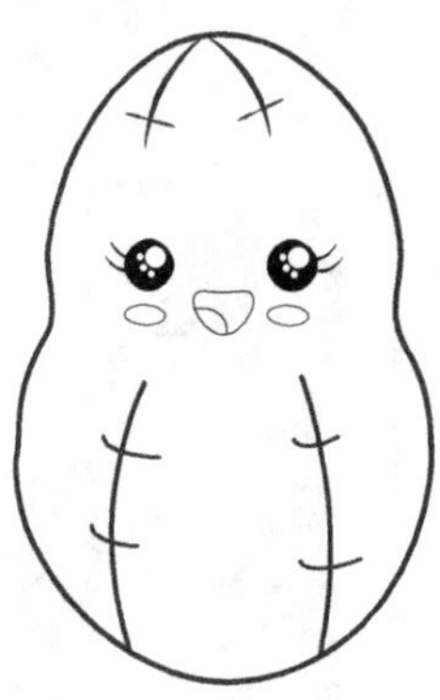

Nn Nn Nn Nn

Nn Nn Nn Nn

Nn Nn Nn Nn

Nn Nn Nn Nn

Nut Nut Nut

Nut Nut Nut

Nut Nut Nut

Nut Nut Nut

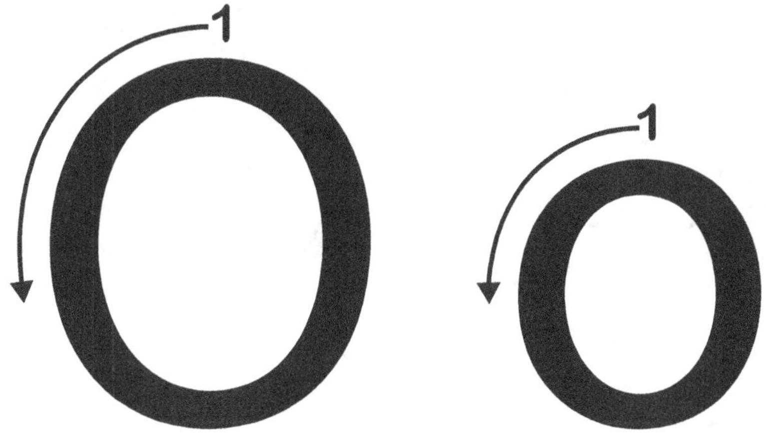

O o is for Orange

Write Alphabet

Oo　　Oo　　Oo　　Oo

Oo　　Oo　　Oo　　Oo

Oo　　Oo　　Oo　　Oo

Oo　　Oo　　Oo　　Oo

Orange　Orange　Orange

Orange　Orange　Orange

Orange　Orange　Orange

Orange　Orange　Orange

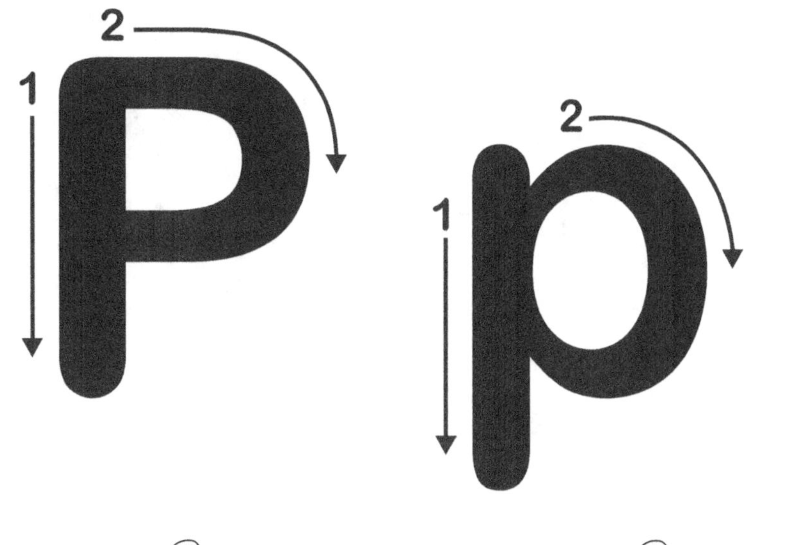

P p is for Pizza

Write Alphabet

Pp   Pp   Pp   Pp

Pp   Pp   Pp   Pp

Pp   Pp   Pp   Pp

Pp   Pp   Pp   Pp

Pizza   Pizza   Pizza

Pizza   Pizza   Pizza

Pizza   Pizza   Pizza

Pizza   Pizza   Pizza

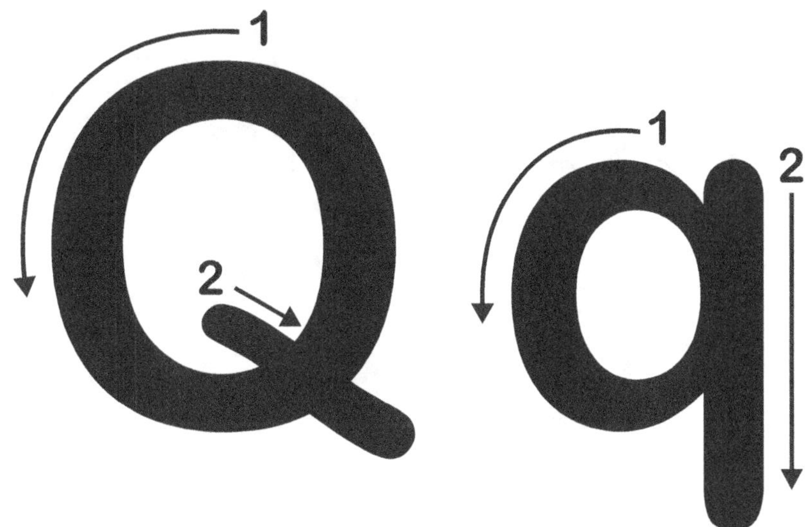

Q Q is for quinoa

Write Alphabet

Qq   Qq   Qq   Qq

Qq   Qq   Qq   Qq

Qq   Qq   Qq   Qq

Qq   Qq   Qq   Qq

quinoa   quinoa   quinoa

quinoa   quinoa   quinoa

quinoa   quinoa   quinoa

quinoa   quinoa   quinoa

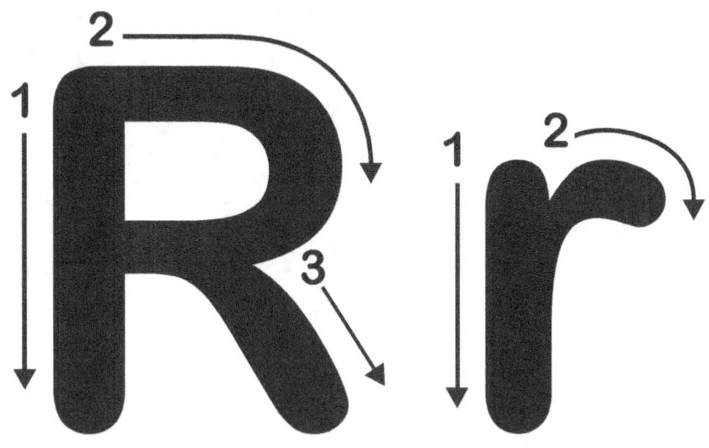

R r is for Rice

Write Alphabet

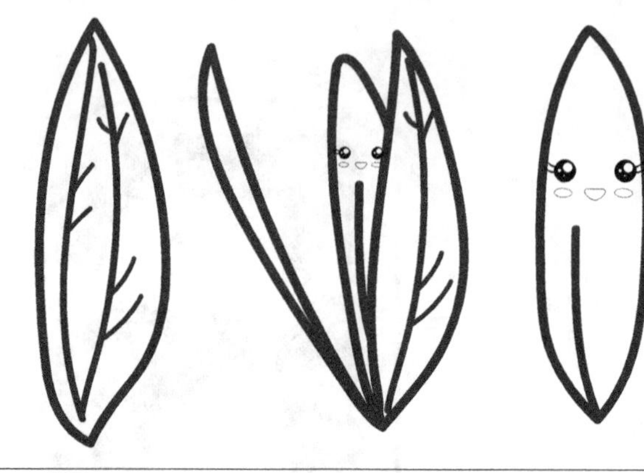

Rr   Rr   Rr   Rr

Rr   Rr   Rr   Rr

Rr   Rr   Rr   Rr

Rr   Rr   Rr   Rr

Rice   Rice   Rice

Rice   Rice   Rice

Rice   Rice   Rice

Rice   Rice   Rice

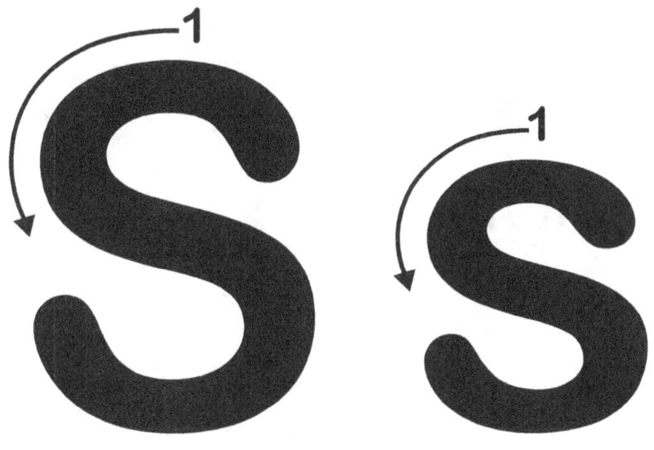

S s is for Sausage

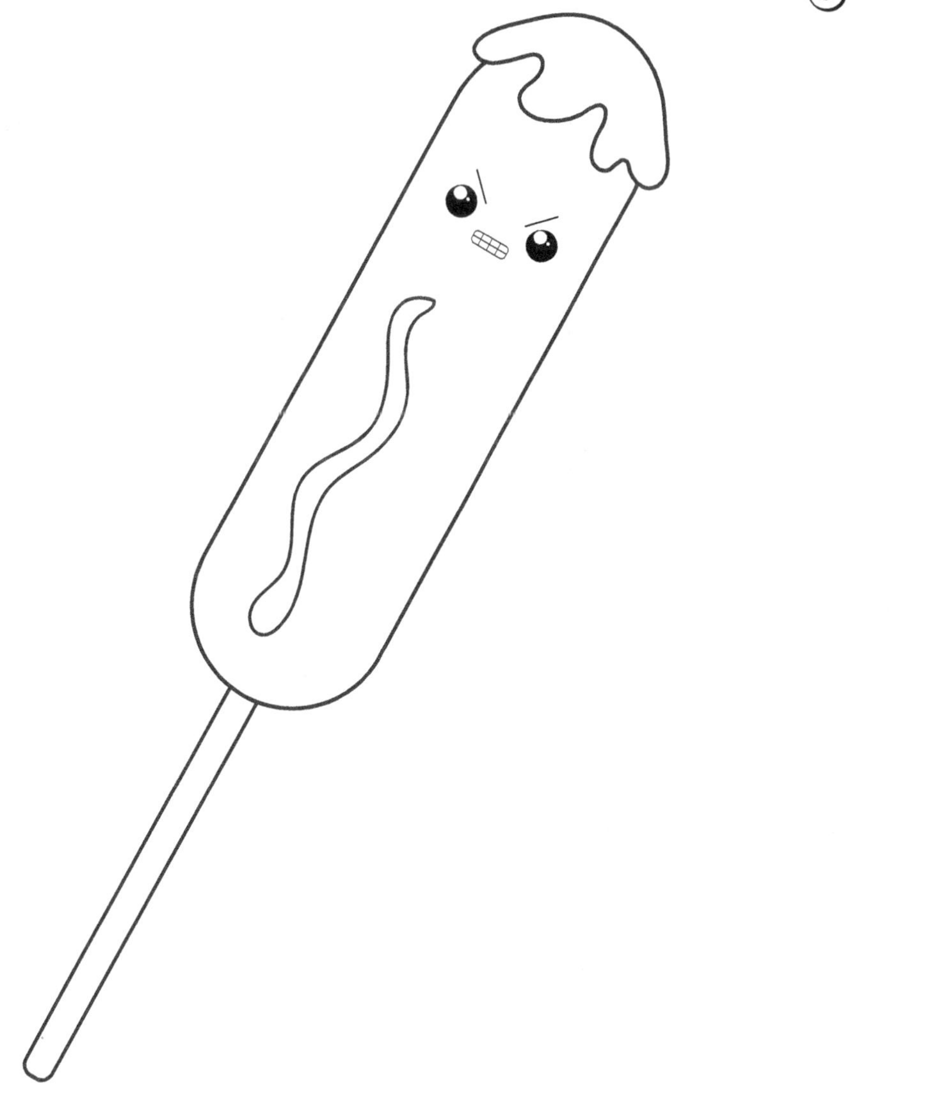

Write Alphabet

Ss   Ss   Ss   Ss

Ss   Ss   Ss   Ss

Ss   Ss   Ss   Ss

Ss   Ss   Ss   Ss

Sausage   Sausage

Sausage   Sausage

Sausage   Sausage

Sausage   Sausage

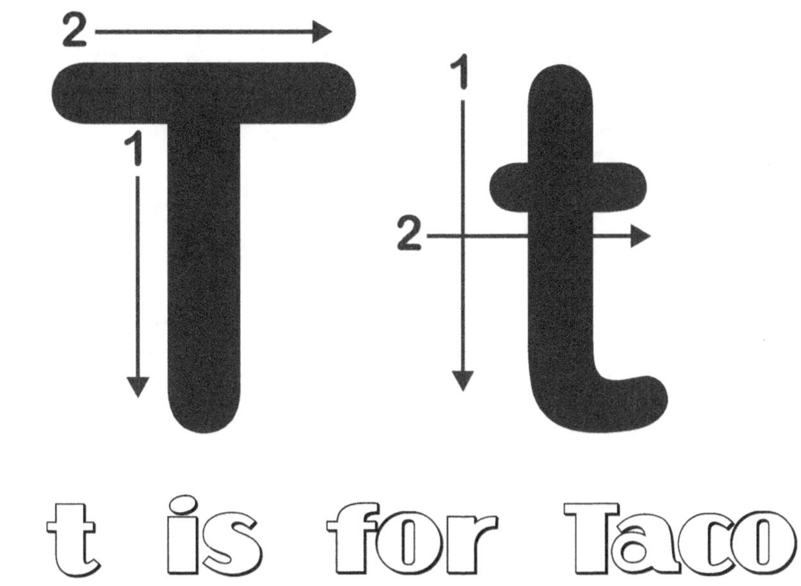

T t is for Taco

Write Alphabet

Tt   Tt   Tt   Tt

Tt   Tt   Tt   Tt

Tt   Tt   Tt   Tt

Tt   Tt   Tt   Tt

Taco   Taco   Taco

Taco   Taco   Taco

Taco   Taco   Taco

Taco   Taco   Taco

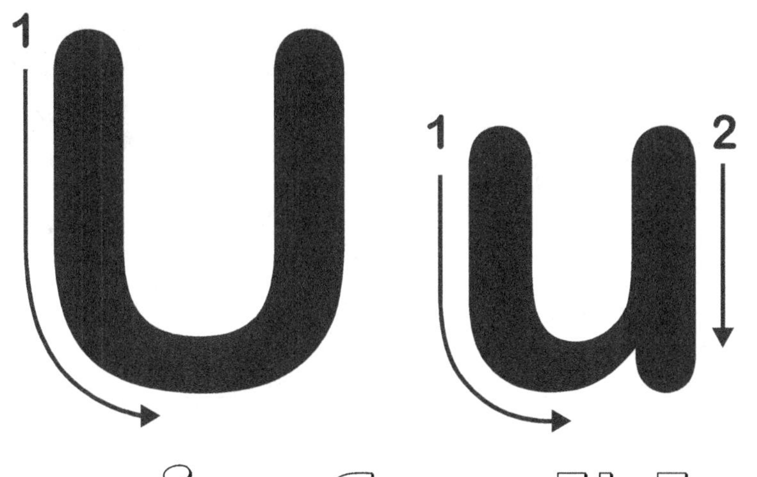

U u is for Udon

Write Alphabet

Uu   Uu   Uu   Uu

Uu   Uu   Uu   Uu

Uu   Uu   Uu   Uu

Uu   Uu   Uu   Uu

Udon   Udon   Udon

Udon   Udon   Udon

Udon   Udon   Udon

Udon   Udon   Udon

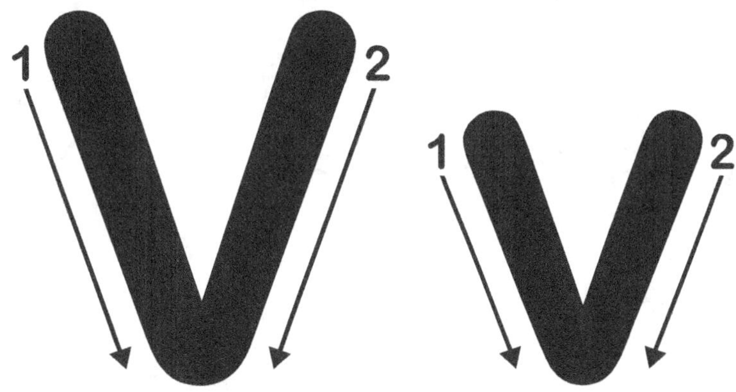

V v is for Vanilla

Write Alphabet

Vv Vv Vv Vv

Vv Vv Vv Vv

Vv Vv Vv Vv

Vv Vv Vv Vv

Vanilla Vanilla Vanilla

Vanilla Vanilla Vanilla

Vanilla Vanilla Vanilla

Vanilla Vanilla Vanilla

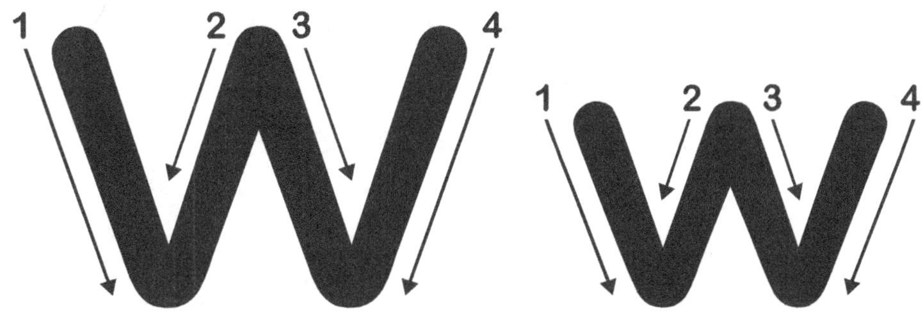

W w is for Watermelon

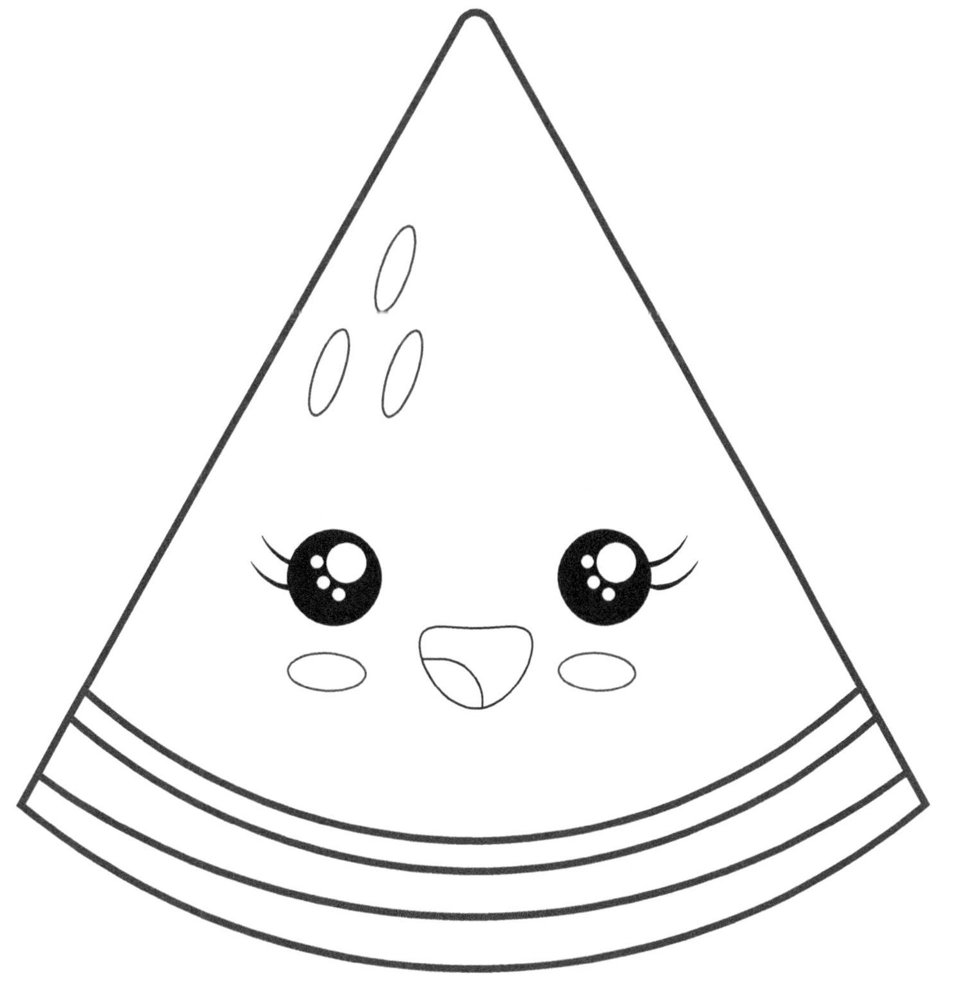

Write Alphabet

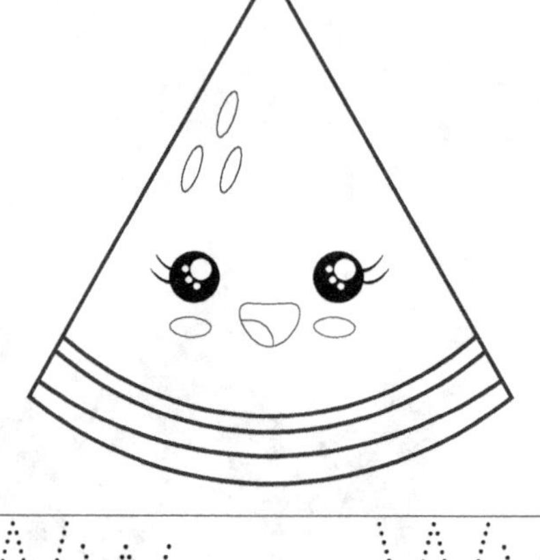

Ww　　Ww　　Ww　　Ww

Ww　　Ww　　Ww　　Ww

Ww　　Ww　　Ww　　Ww

Ww　　Ww　　Ww　　Ww

Watermelon　　Watermelon

Watermelon　　Watermelon

Watermelon　　Watermelon

Watermelon　　Watermelon

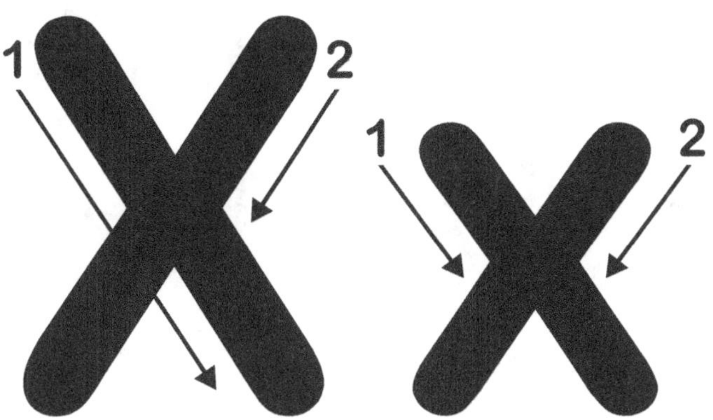

X x is for Ximenia

Write Alphabet

Xx   Xx   Xx   Xx

Xx   Xx   Xx   Xx

Xx   Xx   Xx   Xx

Xx   Xx   Xx   Xx

Ximenia Ximenia Ximenia

Ximenia Ximenia Ximenia

Ximenia Ximenia Ximenia

Ximenia Ximenia Ximenia

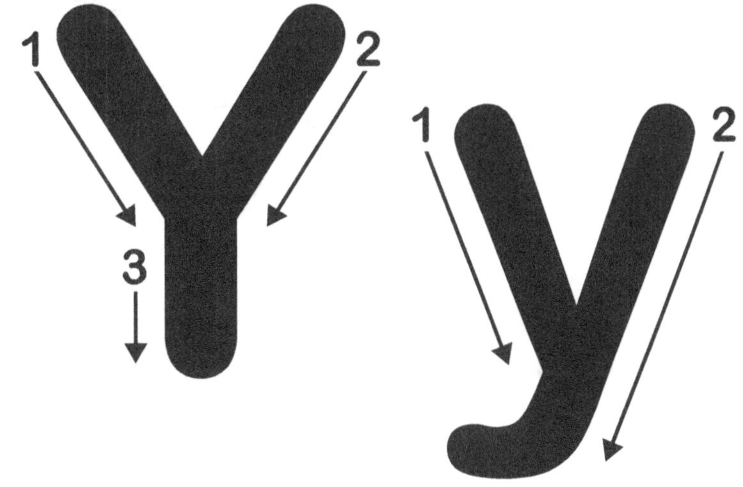

Y y is for Yogurt

Write Alphabet

Yy Yy Yy Yy

Yy Yy Yy Yy

Yy Yy Yy Yy

Yy Yy Yy Yy

Yogurt Yogurt Yogurt

Yogurt Yogurt Yogurt

Yogurt Yogurt Yogurt

Yogurt Yogurt Yogurt

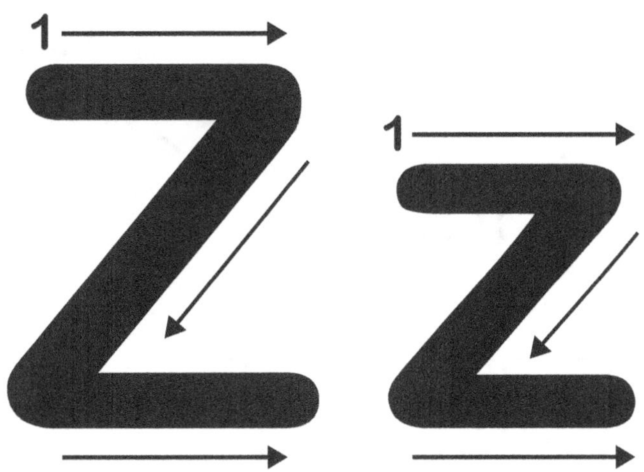

Z z is for Zucchini

Write Alphabet

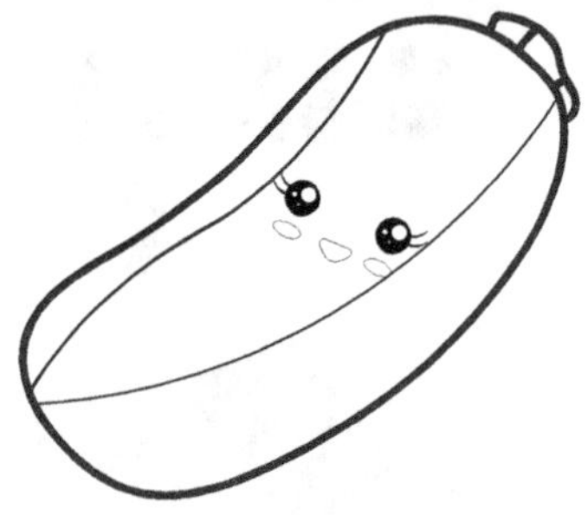

Zz Zz Zz Zz

Zz Zz Zz Zz

Zz Zz Zz Zz

Zz Zz Zz Zz

Zucchini Zucchini Zucchini

Zucchini Zucchini Zucchini

Zucchini Zucchini Zucchini

Zucchini Zucchini Zucchini